THE DOCUMENT

Thank you for attending

I would like yo... ... of our appreciation and, because, ...go when I read it, it became the inspiration for the community relationship we now hope to forge with you, our valued Partners.

Xerox is inviting our Partners to join us on a journey that began three years ago: "The e-Procurement Firestorm".

The event on 25th April will undoubtedly give you a clearer view of the journey we will undertake together.

I believe this book will consolidate and endorse our message by helping you to understand the point from which this journey began.

I hope that it equally inspires you to join the Xerox Europe "Firestorm community" – together we can explore the New World of eProcurement.

[signature]

James F Lawler
Executive Director
Finance, Information Management & Xerox Purchasing, Real
Estate Services & Solutions
Xerox Europe

Xerox Limited
Riverview
Oxford Road
Uxbridge
Middlesex UB8 1HS
Telephone 01895 251133
Fax 01895 254095

REGISTERED OFFICE BRIDGE HOUSE, OXFORD ROAD UXBRIDGE, MIDDLESEX UB8 1HS. REGISTERED IN ENGLAND NO. 575914

THE BATTLE OF THE PORTALS

Thomas Power & George Jerjian

April 2001

About the Authors

Thomas Power

Born in 1964, Thomas qualified as a marketing consultant in 1986 and joined Amstrad plc, where he became Alan Sugar's protégé. He featured prominently in Sugar's book: *The Amstrad Story* (published in 1989). In 1988, he founded and became Managing Director of DMS Europe, a database marketing company, which he sold in 1992 to Urban Science and remained there until 1996. He has a love of databases and mathematics, which he explains, is the core of Electronic Commerce.

In 1994, he sold the world's first geographic market analysis system to Microsoft and in 1995 he sold the world's first real time Internet Auction to Mercedes-Benz (this was before Onsale and eBay). In 1996, he sold the world's first Electronic Commerce Marketplace to BT (British Telecom) while Group Managing Director of TDS Group Ltd.

Today, Thomas is considered a "Thought Leader" by many of his clients and the media have called him an Ecommerce guru. He is a director and Chief Knowledge Officer of www.ecademy.com and co-author of *The E-Business Advantage*, *E-Business to the Power of e* and *Ecosystem: Living the 12 Principles of E-Business*. He is married with three children and lives in Surrey, England.

George Jerjian

Born in 1955, George graduated from Bradford University Management Centre with a degree in Business Studies and a major in Marketing. Over the past twenty years, he has gained enormous experience in different businesses and in different countries. George has worked in the marketing function in the import and export trade, in furniture and interior design, in commercial and residential real estate, in financial services and most recently in e-business. His work has taken him to Africa for two years, in the US for eight and in the UK for some twelve years.

In 1993, George graduated with a master's degree in Journalism from New York University and was awarded first place for his documentary, *"Emerging Airlines: The Kiwi Story"* by The Academy of Television Arts & Sciences (EMMY). In 1996, while working with Allied Dunbar Assurance plc, he wrote *"Seven Ages: Personal Financial Planning"*. In 1999, he wrote *Battle of the Portals*. From July 2001, he launches *Ecosystem: Living the 12 Principles of E-Business*, which is published by FT.com. He is an author, speaker and Chartered Marketer. George is married with two children and lives in London.

Thomas Power
Non-Executive Director,
ROUTECAUSE LTD, UK
Email: thomaspower2@compuserve.com
Mobile: +44 (0) 7976 438 285

George Jerjian
Director, ROUTECAUSE LTD, UK
Email: georgejerjian@lineone.net
Mobile: +44 (0) 7801 106 798

John Bromley
PA to Thomas Power and George Jerjian
Email: brom@freeuk.com
Phone: +44 (0) 1428 645975
Fax: +44 (0) 1428 645794
Mobile: +44 (0) 7970 051862

First published May 1999 by The Ecademy Ltd
Revised April 2001

Copyright © March 1999 George Jerjian and Ecademy Ltd

The rights of George Jerjian and Ecademy Ltd to be identified as the authors of the Work have been asserted by them in accordance with the Copyright, Designs and Patents Act 1988.

All rights reserved. No part of this publication may be reproduced, stored in a retrieval system, or transmitted, in any form or by any means without the prior written permission of both authors, nor be otherwise circulated in any form or binding or cover other than that in which it is being published and without a similar condition being imposed on the subsequent purchaser.

The Battle of the Portals

Introduction		9
One	What is a Portal?	11
Two	How did all this happen so fast?	20
Three	Why a battle? What's at stake?	30
Four	Who's at war?	41
Five	No portal, no comment.	47
Six	Ecosystem: The 12 Principles	53
Seven	Winners and losers.	62
Eight	What's next?	74
Nine	Where's my pocket portal?	83
Ten	Can it still go further?	91
Conclusion		100

Introduction

Thomas Power and I met in December 1998 in the swimming pool lobby of the Schweitzerhof Hotel in Davos, Switzerland. We were both on a skiing holiday with our respective spouses, Penny and Talyn and our children. We went swimming daily to indulge our children and to deplete their inexhaustible energy. Over the week that we spent together, Thomas and I discovered that although we come from different backgrounds, we not only have much in common in our perspectives and visions, but that we could brainstorm effortlessly and at high velocity. Thomas introduced me to the world of electronic commerce and I impressed him with my communications skills.

On returning to London, we resumed our meetings and I accompanied him to a number of Ecommerce related meetings. We then decided to write a book together. Over a period of ninety days, Thomas flooded my brain with the history, the economics, the innovations, current developments of Ecommerce and what he perceives as the end game in this "Battle of the Portals." I read and perused sixty books on the subject, endless newspaper and magazine articles and when I was ready, I decided to take a week off work to write the first draft of the book.

With privacy and peace as necessities to execute this work, I decided to spend that week at a monastery. In my teens, I had gone to Douai School in Berkshire County, in England (not Massachusetts). Douai was a Catholic boarding school run by monks of the Benedictine Order. These monks had separate living quarters that connected to the school and to the
Abbey. In the last week of March, I spent a gruelling but peaceful week writing the first draft of this book in one of the Abbey guestrooms.

In this revision (April 2001), I have left the text unchanged. What I changed however is Chapter Six, because the Ecommandments have now become Principles and I have found a better way to express and explain them. The object being that the story remains intact and valid, even if some of the information and details are now part of an ongoing and unfolding history.

From 2001, we are setting course for an individual to be able to login any where in the world on any device, with a single user name and password. Is it any wonder that AOL is protesting to the US Government that Microsoft is once again exercising its monopoly power with its single user ID or 'passport'?

George Jerjian
London
April 2001

Chapter One
What Is a Portal?

History

The origin of the word derives from the Latin, *porta*, meaning a gate or doorway to a city. The city is Rome, which at its height had as many as 19 portals, with names like Porta Appia, Porta Praetoria and Porta Salaria, which will please the historians among you. In fact the word city derives from the Latin word, *civitas*, meaning community, which is what the Internet represents at a different level. Within Rome, distinctive communities developed around each portal, because each portal was a medium in itself. An Internet Portal is all encompassing in its potential. It is a combination of the following: a friend, a counsellor, a buyer, a companion, an influencer, a doorway to the network, a broker, an infomediary, an 'electronic relationship manager' and 'guardian of your personal information' from abuse by the brands. A portal is certainly a gate or a doorway to the Internet. It is also a vein with tributaries that conveys data and information to and from a Portal. But it is also much more than this

Today

Portals are web sites that are used as launch pads for customers looking to surf the Web. Examples of current Portals are AOL (America On Line) Yahoo MSN (Microsoft Network), Lycos, Disney/Go and Excite.
Amazon and Altavista (owned by Compaq) are not as yet portals, but they are certainly heading in that direction. In fact, we expect Amazon will acquire or merge with Yahoo and emerge under our code names of Yamazon or Amazoo! (Notice also that Rupert Murdoch at News International has a very keen eye on placing Yahoo on the end of all his cable networks). Although most will have started life in different guises, they will evolve into Portals by virtue of the fact that they have electronic relationships with their customers. The list is not definitive and there are still many portals that will come on board before the cost of starting up becomes prohibitive, we currently estimate the cost of catching up AOL, Amazon or Yahoo at between $2bn and $5bn! The cost is least for those who started early and from that universe will emerge the "Coke" and the "Pepsi" of the Portals.

Opportunity

These Portals are not just there to help people manage the Internet. The Portal proprietors have realised that their Portals can make people's lives easier and by so doing they can make a great deal of money. Their aim is to do that through personalisation;[1] getting people to tell them about themselves and then using that data in creative ways to provide a useful service to each and everyone of us as individuals.

Valuations of Relationships

The value of portals today is not about what they are selling or even about their balance sheets. It is about the customers that have perhaps used them in some cases or even bought a product or service and come on board. It's all about building databases - customer relationship databases. Unlike the traditional relationships with customers, which tend to be physical or via the telephone, or mail, these relationships with customers are 'electronic'. So what's new? Well, electronic relationships are much more powerful than traditional relationships because over time, the databases that manage these electronic relationships 'learn' individual behaviour and so make them intelligent. With these intelligent databases there is no room for human error, inconsistency or sloth. As a result profits can be maximised. How else can you explain the phenomenal growth of Amazon.com, which has in excess of 8 million fanatically loyal customers and whose market capitalisation is about $30 billion and is expected to grow tenfold within the next 36 months?

We believe that the strategy of the Portals is to become global supermarkets, providing everything for an individual, at home, at work and on the move. They are in fact the new Public Utilities.

Amazon

Let's look at a much-used example of Amazon. It is much more than the "Earth's Biggest Bookstore." It is one of the most comprehensive retail experiences on the Web. If you have already ordered from them, please continue reading. If you haven't, then do so now and order any book you like [www.amazon.com in the US or www.amazon.co.uk in the UK or www.amazon.de in Germany or www.amazon.fr in France]. It is an experience, which no amount of reading can replace. Not only is it convenient to order on line rather than go to a bookshop, but also in most cases it is also less expensive, even after accounting for the transport charges.

There is no theoretical limit to the number of books a virtual store can carry (Amazon had 3 million titles listed by mid 1998 and 125,000 CD titles and it was also listing titles from independent publishers whose books had never made it into the bookshops.) Amazon's designers understood that bookstore customers are in two moods: browsing or hunting for a particular book. You can search by author, by title, by ISBN, by special subject, by words or categories or recommended lists of critics and specialists. Not only are authors invited to submit their own interviews, but readers are also invited to add their own reviews - a formidable feedback. Amazon calls their community of customers -Amazonians. The electronic relationship they are developing with their customers is becoming tribal much like sports fans that follow one specific team.

You can either drop your selected books in a shopping basket and pay at the end when you are ready to leave or you can buy your books with one-click of your mouse. In either case, your payments and deliveries can be consolidated into one. In case you are wondering about security of your credit card, we write about it in Chapter 6. After you place the order, Amazon emails you a confirmation in minutes and advises when you should receive the book, normally within 48 hours. When the book is dispatched the following day, you receive another email advising you. It is not only refreshing to get that kind of service, but it is a truly pleasing experience. Under account maintenance, you have a special password to let you in and change any details on your account. You can also have a look at all the orders you ever placed with them, in full detail. [2]

Let's look at the cost side of the equation. A cyber bookshop or a bookshop on the Web pays relatively less for the costs of high traffic. It does not have high rental costs of buildings associated with prime locations. Lastly, it has an advantage in lower payroll costs compared to physical bookshops: but let's not ignore the fact that Amazon has 3,000 employees. What's more, this cyber bookshop receives immediate payment from its customers and does not have to pay the publisher for some months. What a war chest to fight and win the largest number of customers!

Privacy, what privacy?

If customers realise that these Portals want to build customer relationship databases, will they not withhold information? Certainly, you would think. In reality, the answer is sometimes, no. Look at Free-PC.com. In early 1999, they offered a free personal computer to individuals who registered at their site and were prepared to complete a ten-minute application form. These individuals would also have to accept advertisements all around their screen and all their enquiries, browsing and purchases would be monitored and studied over time. Over one million two hundred thousand individuals have applied for a free personal computer demonstrating that "free lunches" can sometimes overcome privacy. This does go to show that PCs connected to the Internet should be given away in much the same way that mobile phones were in the recent past. It is the vendors or the brands that should pay for the privilege to sell to prime consumers. Notice how in the UK, Murdoch's BSkyB have responded to this by offering their cable TV set-top boxes for free also with free internet access.

Time

Privacy is not the only problem facing the consumer. Time is more important for most of us. Telephone calls, real mail, electronic mail, faxes and mobile phones and even people are besieging us all. We cannot get on with our work, without constant interruptions. We are experiencing 'time famine' [3] and coupled with this, we, as consumers, have to make decisions on an explosion of choices and complex products. As if this is not enough of a drag on our time, the Internet itself is becoming so congested with information that it can take a great deal of our time to find the information we need. We believe that this widening gap will open an opportunity for an agent or broker or intermediary to help process and manage the information and time for the customer at home, at work or on the move. In *Net Worth*, authors John Hagel and Marc Singer, call this agent - an "infomediary."

Infomediary – "at your service"

An infomediary, although such a creature does not yet exist, will be a company that will play the custodian, agent and broker of customers' information (arguably Equifax and Experian could perform this role). With the customer's approval, it will market it to vendors (or suppliers) on behalf of the consumers, while at the same time protecting their privacy and potentially passing on monies received from vendors for the selected information given. The infomediary will allow access of information to the vendors without revealing the identity of the customer. The infomediary will have to inspire confidence and trust, much like a lawyer should. Infomediaries will also provide consumers with the best of both worlds: lower interaction costs and increased privacy. This will stem from their ability to build an extraordinarily deep and broad informational profile of consumers. This in turn will enable the infomediary to lower the consumers' high communication costs on the Web. Lastly, this customer profile will prove irresistible to vendors. The vendors will benefit also, because instead of throwing away their monies on mail shots, telephone calls and emails, they will be able to reduce their costs and pass on the difference to their customers.

The more value vendors learn to deliver to customers in return for access to information, the more willing infomediaries' clients will be to let them have that access. And the more access vendors have, the more value they will be able to deliver, and so on. [4]

Let's just suppose you are an American Express travel agent and you have a young couple in their early thirties, no children, sitting in front of you, who want to go on holiday somewhere in the Caribbean. Clearly the more information you can secure about them, the better chance you will have of satisfying their holiday desires. Let's suppose you had access to detailed information about them including their individual annual income and expenditure, their shopping and eating habits, their hobbies and their likes and dislikes. Suppose you also know their good and bad experiences on holiday, at home and at work and their virtues and their vices. You could tailor a holiday for them that would virtually guarantee they come back to you, because you have increased their chances of a successful holiday and reduced the chances of a bad holiday – all because the information you had was detailed, fresh and appropriate for your customers.

It's the Portal or Infomediary that will save us time and protect our privacy from vendors. They are the new public utilities; they are the new brands we will become dependant on. They will become our (electronic) personal assistants available on all devices PC, TV, mobile phone, handheld computer, telephone and so on.

Chapter Two
How did All This Happen So Fast?

The answer is technology. This is a general term for the processes by which human beings fashion tools and machines to increase their control and understanding of the material environment.

Technology in itself is not the issue. In fact, many of the technologies in the last 150 years have taken about 30 or so years from inception to introduction to the market; for instance, the railways, the telephone, the wireless (radio) and television. The issue is the rate at which this technology changes and develops its own momentum. Innovations now seem to appear at a rate that increases exponentially, without respect to geographical limits or political systems. You may remember the "glasnost" reforms introduced by President Gorbachev brought about a coup d'etat against him during which all communications were severed. The coup failed because Gorbachev's forces had access to mobile phones; technology saved the day. For those of us born after 1960, these technological changes have already changed our way of life with unexpected social consequences.

These changes are set to continue at ever increasing speeds.

Comparison to nature

Before we continue to expand on technological changes, let's look at an appropriate comparison with geological changes. Jeff Bezos, head of Amazon.com gives us that when he compares the rise of the Internet to the Cambrian era in evolution (540 million years ago): "That was when the earth had the greatest rate of new life. What people don't know is that it also had the greatest rate of extinction." [5] Clearly, the causes of the extinction are not clear, but they may be related to changing climate and exceptionally low sea level: much the same reasons given for the extinction of the dinosaurs. The secret of survival is captured in a quote attributed to Charles Darwin: "It is not the strongest of the species that survive, nor the most intelligent, but those most responsive to change." In other words, adaptability assures survival, nothing more, nothing less.

So where did this technology start?

The remit of this book does not allow us to go back in detail at the historical origin of technology, but a cursory look will help to put things in perspective.

The earliest technology dates from about 250,000 BC with nomadic groups of hunters, who discovered the first tools, such as axes, knives and other instruments. The next big step came with the control of fire. This did not just bring warmth and light; it brought about baking clay pots and pottery and all the processes that fire combined with other technologies creates for us today. Between 10,000 and 5000 BC, agriculture was on the rise and farming communities developed in the Near East. There is evidence to show that two-wheeled carts and wooden boats were constructed and used in Mesopotamia around 3500 BC. [6]

After about 4000 BC one of the most complex creations of humankind appeared: the city. The city itself is a technological system. The first written symbols to describe a city is a circle containing networks of lines that indicate transportation and communications systems – not unlike a portal on the Internet. Urbanisation also stimulated a greater need for writing. The first cities were also in effect war machines, built within walls for defence and organised for battle and conquest, just for a moment we would like you to consider this clause, *"organised for battle and conquest",* in light of what is happening with today's Portals. This was followed by military technology, which came in different stages: the army, the chariot, and the cavalry. The Greeks became a power because of their shipbuilding skills; Alexander the Great defeated the Persians, in part, because of his naval power. The Romans were great technologists. Roman engineers built over 44,000 miles (70,000 km) of roads across their vast empire (their network) and built arches, gateways or portals into their cities. They also introduced the watermill and waterwheel and in the military context, they improved weapons such as the javelin and catapult. The Middle Ages were not dark in terms of technology; they were very adaptive. The windmill, the spinning wheel, the horseshoe, the clock and the printing press were all innovations of the Middle Ages and they were far from insignificant. [6]

In fact it has been said that the printing press was directly and indirectly responsible for destroying the hegemony of the Roman Catholic Church in Europe. [7]

The Industrial Revolution started in England and the first textile factories appeared in 1740, concentrating on textile production. At that time, the majority of English people wore woollen garments, but within a century, the scratchy woollens were replaced by cotton, especially after the 1793 invention of the cotton gin by Eli Whitney, an American. By 1805, Joseph-Marie Jacquard devised a method for automated weaving that is the precursor to early computer technology. The looms are directed by instructions on a series of punched cards. Other English inventions such as the flying shuttle and carding machines of John Kay, the water frame of Richard Arkwright, the spinning jenny of James Hargreaves and the improvements in weaving made by Samuel Crompton were all integrated with a new source of power, the steam engine. In England, Thomas Newcomen, James Watt, and Richard Trevithick and in the U.S. Oliver Evans developed the steam engine. Between the 1790s and the 1830s, a period of 40 years, there were more than 100,000 power looms with 10 million spindles in England. This revolution created the modern factory. The ultimate assembly of a product was not the work of one person but the result of an integrated, corporate system. An interesting similarity can be discerned between the steam engine then and the Internet today. The steam engine integrated several of the existing technologies in much the same way that the Internet is now harnessing the telephone, the mobile (cell phone), the radio, the television and of course the PC.

Increased Pace of Innovation

It took several hundred thousand years to transform how man uses instruments to work and build a life. In the recent past, it took decades for instruments of communication to become available to the population at large. Yet today, innovations are being produced on a daily basis.

In 1876, Alexander Graham Bell produced the first telephone capable of transmitting and receiving human speech with quality and timbre; early devices had appeared in the 1850s and were capable of transmitting sounds but not voices. In 1900, the world saw the start of the mass production of automobiles and in 1903, Orville Wright flew the first aeroplane.

In 1921, the mass production of the radio started, even though the first human voice was heard on the telegraph as early as 1906. According to UNESCO (The United Nations Scientific and Cultural Organisation) more than 1.6 billion radios are now in use in the world (worth noting as we believe no more than 2 billion people will ever be connected to the Internet). That means nearly one for every three people; however, three out of four is found in Europe and North America. Although radio mass production started 40 years before, by 1960 only 7% of the world's nations had one radio for every five people; by the late 1980s a majority had.

In 1946, the mass production of television started, even though television had been available since 1927 and made its dramatic debut in 1939. Because of the much higher costs for television production and receivers, its broadcasting development lags behind that of the radio. Of more than 750 million television sets in the world, roughly 80% are concentrated in Europe, North America and Japan. In most developing countries television is limited to the major urban areas. In the U.S., 98% of all households have a television and almost 100% have a radio. In the early 1990s, about 62% of all U.S. households were connected to cable TV, with most providing in excess of 30 channels.

Computer mass production started in 1953, although it was back in 1940 that the world's first operational computer, known as Robinson, was created by the British and succeeded in decoding messages from Enigma, the Nazis' first-generation enciphering machine. By 1943, the British computer team built Colossus, using electric tubes that are 100 to 1000 times faster than relays used by Robinson. This ultimately contributed to the Allied victory because it could decipher complex German codes. Forty years later, in October 1981, IBM introduced the personal computer. Together with clones from Compaq, Dell and others, within 8 years 200 million personal computers had been sold. In 1982, Lotus, a software manufacturer, introduced its "1-2-3" spreadsheets. This was later taken over by Microsoft's Excel. In 1984, Apple Computer's Macintosh introduced the concept of operating on WIMP (windows, icons, mouse and pointer) based on the creations at Xerox Parc in Palo Alto. WIMP made working on the computer easier for everyone and soon made the cumbersome DOS (disk operating system) obsolete. After six years in the "Windows" wilderness (1985-91), Microsoft introduced its Windows 3.1 version in 1991. Then came the full office applications such as Microsoft's' Office. In 1994, Netscape introduced the Internet Browser named Navigator, which Microsoft replicated with its Internet Explorer and so the innovation continues. By 1999 both companies had released their fifth versions of the Browser. Microsoft is often regarded as the master follower in the marketplace, so let us never rule out its final position in the Battle of the Portals.

Facsimile machines had been used for over a decade at U.S. Post Offices, before someone discovered that it could be marketed to the general public.
In the 1980s, it was illegal in the United States to send a fax message because the U.S. Post Office claimed an ancient monopoly. An edict to that effect was issued, but was clearly unenforceable.

Lastly, the Internet was introduced in 1958, when the U.S. Department of Defence formed ARPA, the Advanced Research Projects Agency to have an edge over the Soviet Union. In 1969 this spawned the ARPAnet - a military research network. A decade later, research agencies and universities flocked to join the Internet. The 1970s saw the introduction of electronic mail and by 1986 the Internet Relay Chat burst onto the scene. [8] In 1991, America On Line (AOL) started its business as an Internet service provider and in 1995, Yahoo started out as a search engine on the Internet.

The above transformations are visible and more obvious. There are other less obvious ones, not immediately connected, that lie just beneath the surface. These are equally important in driving innovation forward because they provide the multiplier effect. Among these are automation, databases, transistors and the law of accelerating returns.

The Multiplier Effects

1.   *Automation* is a subject that Adam Smith touched on as early as 1776 in his *Wealth of Nations*, which includes the division of labour, mechanisation and feedback. Automation in industry greatly increased production and lowered costs thereby making cars, refrigerators, televisions, and telephones available to more people. Automation has also had a major influence in the modern office. Personal computers are used as word processors and this technology combines a small computer with a display screen, a typewriter keyboard and printer. As you know, it is used to edit texts, to type form letters tailored to the recipient and to manipulate mailing lists and other data. This system has increased office productivity and reduced unit costs.

2.   *Databases* are any collection of data organised for storage in a computer memory and designed for easy access by authorised users. This aspect is one of the most important components in the battle that Portals are

currently waging because they hold the full customer information history. Without it, there is no business.

3.   *Transistors* are the common name for a group of electronic devices used as amplifiers or oscillators in communications, control and computer systems. Bell Laboratories developed them in 1948 and during the late 1960s a new electronic technique, the Integrated Circuit, began to replace the transistor. Although roughly the same size as a transistor, it can perform the functions of 15 to 20 transistors. Large scale integrated circuits followed in the early 1970s as a natural development and the so-called microprocessor came in the mid 1970s as a further refinement. Gordon Moore, the founder of Intel (Integrated Electronics) Corporation, the microchip manufacturer, proclaimed Moore's law in 1964, which states that "the power of microprocessors (transistors) doubles very 24 months." This was revised down to 18 months and has been revised downwards in months ever since, as microprocessors seem to become ever faster, ever quicker.

4.   *"The law of accelerating returns"* can be explained in the following mathematical example. The value of a network goes up as the square of the number of users. If the value of a network to a single user is £1 for each other user on the network, then a network of size 10 has a total value of £100. In contrast, a network of size 100 has a total of £10,000. A tenfold increase in the size of the network leads to a hundredfold increase in its value. This is known as Metcalfe's law. [9]

"Exponential growth is the result of the doubling of microprocessor power every 18 months (Moore's law) multiplied by the value of a network which goes up as the square of the number of users (Metcalfe's law)"

Chapter Three
Why a battle? What's at stake?

Alliances

Industry analysts say that clearer battle lines are being drawn in the struggle for commercial dominance of the World Wide Web. Every week, a new set of hot interest IPOs (Initial Public Offerings) bring new entrants of Portals, auction sites, web communities, and electronic commerce technologies to the investment universe. Wall Street's appetite is insatiable and it is devouring any company that can add the word ".com". The reason is that a once disparate and fragmented medium is forming into a series of alliances; alliances centred on a combination of global entertainment giants and "new media" blue chips, which now muster higher valuations than their counterparts (eBay.com recently acquired traditional auction house Butterfield & Butterfield). In late 1998, Disney has linked up with Infoseek and its ABC News sites and launched the Go Network. America Online (AOL) has struck a major deal with CBS. Lycos, the second largest search engine's link with USA Network, the home shopping empire may be coming apart. Excite, its rival, is likely to become the portal for AT&T, @Home and its cable divisions, TCI (and maybe soon Mediaone too) and Time Warner has already owned CNN for some time.

Media analysts say that these alliances are predicated on the classic media business model; gathering and packaging audiences for advertisers with the long run view of creating environments that will be a hybrid of a mega-mall and theme park. These Ecommerce alliances or Portals are the new global public utilities, which plan to retain web surfers within a universe they control, thus maximising sales commissions and advertising revenue. This means assembling the widest possible range of products, services, entertainment, auctions and lifestyle so as to induce the surfer to stay online for as long as possible. It is no longer about "one-stop-shopping"; it's about "one-stop-living". [10]

Whether it's about "one-stop-shopping" or about "one-stop-living", there are two crucial questions to ask: 1) Will these Portals be on the side of the vendors or the consumers? And 2) are they intermediaries or infomediaries?

The answer to the first question, we believe, is that the Portals will be on the side of the consumer. This is not for altruistic reasons or for public relations, but because the consumer or customer or electronic relationship, call them what you will, is their real asset around whom all business revolves and without whom there is no business. Vendors, employees and even shareholders appreciate this fact as evidenced by the value that Wall Street is placing on these relationships. For instance Yahoo has some 35 million electronic relationships with customers and has a market capitalisation of $35bn, valuing each relationship at $1,000. On the other end of the scale, Internet auction web site eBay has 4 million electronic relationships with buyers and sellers and a market capitalisation of $28bn, valuing each relationship at $7,000. The customer relationship is what Wall Street considers the most important asset of these Internet companies. The customer is, at last, truly, the king!

As to the second question, are they intermediaries or infomediaries, we believe, they are infomediaries. An intermediary is generally human and acts as a go-between or an agent, and often collects commission from the vendor on sales. There is always the possibility that intermediaries may have a conflict of interest, particularly if the customer is not giving them much business. Do they provide the best deal for the customer or the best commission rate for their business? The infomediary does not have the same conflict of interest. First it is non-human and it will surf the net and find the best deal for its customer. Secondly, it will not jeopardise the relationship, because so much business depends on it.

Six alliances have already taken shape and although they are still in their infancy, there are unlikely to be many more - despite the determination of those left on the sidelines to get into the game. Few of the web alliances have been forged by acquisition. Those that do, end up as mergers, as the older partner is unable to control. A few years ago, many assumed that the entertainment conglomerates would snap up the big portals, but their valuations grew too quickly to the point that the Time Warner's and Viacom's of the world could not afford them. As at February 1999 at a valuation of $35billion, Yahoo is now half the size of Murdoch's global empire. Web media alliances are not entirely a new phenomenon; in 1996, Microsoft and General Electric's NBC established MSNBC, a cable TV channel and web site.

In May 1999, Microsoft invested some $6bn in strategic deals with AT&T and wireless carrier Nextel. It has started a full assault in wiring up Europe. It has bought substantial stakes and continues to forge new partnerships in cable properties in the UK and Netherlands and is investing in France and Portugal. Microsoft is attempting to adapt, in the Darwinian sense, and its objective, as evidenced by its recent alliances, is clearly to place itself in a pre-eminent position, possibly emerging in the "Coke" spot in this new world of electronic commerce.

Which alliances will emerge as the leaders is difficult to say, but what is certain is that a battle is being waged and what's at stake is "customers"- perhaps your customers?

Customers are at stake

There are a little over six billion people on this planet and by 2002, two billion people and 100 million companies will be wired to the Internet. This will create a $5 trillion global online economy ($3trn in the U.S, $1trn in the EU and $1trn in Asia), equivalent to more than half the current GDP output of the U.S or EU economies (both are $8 trillion). The remaining four billion people on the planet will be too young, too old, too (economically) poor or too remote to get connected. The battle is for customers - nothing new there - what is new and different is the fact that unlike traditional connections, the electronic relationships are more powerful because they 'learn' individual behaviour and then respond to it. The battle therefore is to capture as many of the pool of two billion people because the more electronic relationships they capture, the higher is their market capitalisation (remember Wall Street is valuing a Customer Relationship anywhere from $200 to $7000 each). In other words the Portal with the biggest database wins the game! A reminder, currently Yahoo's $35bn market capitalisation can be explained by their 35 million-visitor database, which translates to $1,000 per electronic customer relationship.

Once again, traditional connections were limited to some eight working hours and also limited to the geographical location. With electronic relationships, its 24 hours, 7 days a week, 365 days a year, it's all the time, real time, irrespective of geographical location. Although, this may destroy jobs on one hand, on the other, it will invariably create three shifts round the clock for all businesses, potentially and ultimately creating global full employment.

How do you retain your customers?

The simple answer is making it easy for your customers to work with you; for instance allowing the customer to order with a one-click system. You will also need to make it easier for your suppliers to do business with you; for instance, allowing them to continuously update your stock, within given parameters.

Patricia Seybold, founder of a strategy and technology consulting firm, based in Boston, Massachusetts, and a computer industry consultant for more than twenty years advises that focusing on your existing customers is the winning formula. We highly recommend her book, _Customers.com: How to create a profitable business strategy on the Internet._ [11] As an overview, Seybold states the following five steps to success in electronic commerce:

1. Make it easy for customers to do business with you
2. Focus on the end customer for your products and services
3. Redesign your customer-facing business processes from the end customer's point of view.
4. Wire your company for profit and design an ecommerce architecture
5. Foster customer loyalty

The following three stories, selected from Seybold's book, give a general illustration of what she means.

1. American Airlines (AA).

In 1994, AA saw an opportunity to provide a better service and reduce costs at the same time. It targeted its most loyal customers, the 32 million AAdvantage members and found that just fewer than 90% of them had computers at work or at home.

They introduced a Website on which just about any questions a traveller would ask has an answer. By early

1996 an email service was introduced offering specials fares, discounts fares and savings fares. Within a month they had 20,000 subscribers, within a couple of months it rose to 100,000 and by the end of the year it had mounted to just under 800,000 subscribers. AA next added online transactions: booking your tickets electronically so that you could change it at the last minute if you wanted and earning bonus frequent-flyer miles. AA also sends confirmation each time a booking is made.

The result of AA's efforts is that in the first quarter of 1998, they had already doubled the 1997 revenues and to put it into perspective website bookings at the time represented only 1% of AA's total revenues. Also the online bookings are by far the least expensive and most profitable tickets AA sells.

2. Wells Fargo (WF)

A San Francisco-based banking group, whose online banking services is its fastest growing part of the business. Its clients typically had several accounts and a number of different banking relationships. They wanted to be treated like customers, not bank accounts. So WF piloted a scheme whereby on punching in an individual social security number, all the information on that client would come up. Within three months the pilot project was completed and in December 1993, this system went live.

The second step for WF was to install a firewall as part of bank security, when external email was launched. By

1994, WF was looking at the personal computer as an electronic commerce solution and in March 1995, WF decided to offer banking services via the net. By February 1996, WF customers could transfer funds from one account to another and pay their credit bills. WF next strategic weapon was the automatic bill presentment and moving its customers from credit cards to smart cards. This would speed the time and reduce the cost of transactions by virtue of the fact that the information, detail or monies are on the smart card and do not have to travel down networks to obtain the information.

The result of WF efforts was as follows: from 1989 to 1995 some 20,000 customers took advantage of this offer. By the end of 1996, WF had 300,000 on-line banking customers. By mid-1998, this had increased to just fewer than 500,000.

Online banking customers are more profitable because they are more loyal. According to Frederick Reicheld (author of *The Loyalty Factor*), loyal customers are more profitable because:

> 1) The longer you retain them, the more money you make
> 2) They cost less to serve
> 3) They invest more in your products
> 4) They cross-sell and up-sell themselves
> 5) They generate referrals.

3. PhotoDisc (PD)

This Seattle-based company markets and distributes royalty-free digital stock equipment. Its customers are graphic design professionals in design firms, advertising agencies, publications, and businesses' marketing and communications departments, who need rapid, affordable access to commercial quality photographs and imagery they can use in design projects.

The traditional way was to purchase stock from agencies, which represent the work of professional photographers; but photographs were licensed for one time use and ranged from $100 to $10,000 and they had stringent limitations on photo manipulation. What made it more difficult was that selection of photographs was made by description over the telephone and a follow-up of a colour proof.

PD founders decided to develop a friction-free business. They licensed digitally scanned professional-quality photographs for an affordable price of $20 to $200, allowing unlimited use and photo manipulation. PD launched its first set of digitised photographs on floppy disks in 1991 and on CD-ROM in January 1992 containing 400 photographs priced at $300. It worked. By 1994, their customers started to become involved in designing home pages on the web and wanted to download digital images directly to their computers via the Internet. So PD went live in June 1995 and it allowed people to search by category, browse online and order catalogues. By mid-1995, it also introduced searches by key words, view thumbnail size images, put them in a shopping cart and once payment had been received, download the images electronically from the site. This site was a big hit with the publishing community and from September 1995, PD was selling and delivering its products via the Internet.

One of the first things that PD did when they first started was to build customer profiles, which also included such information as tracking all searches and purchases the customers made. This was then converted into a data mart and analysed by the Content Procurement and the Marketing departments. They were then able to segment their customers and customise emails to them offering specials that would appeal to them. PD also changed its back-end accounting systems to give its customers the reporting flexibility they needed such as to bill the cost of individual images to different clients. Other improvements such as the ability to search images based on colour, composition, structure and texture were added, together with a more refined key word searching, which could be done because each of the photographs was tagged with twenty to thirty key words.

The result was that PD's revenue grew from $28 million in 1996 to $42 million in 1997. By mid-1998, PD's sales were already at $26 million. Sales via the web represented 10% of revenues in 1996, 18% in 1997 and 32% in 1998. The cost was originally budgeted at $150,000; two years later they had spent $2 million and continued to invest.

In mid-1997, UK-based Getty Communications purchased PD for a generous stock plus cash deal. The combined collection of Getty Images, as it is now known, includes 25 million images and 9,500 hours of film footage.

In her book, Seybold highlights the eight critical success factors:

1. Target the right customers
2. Own the customer's total experience
3. Streamline business processes
4. Provide a 360-degree view of the customer relationship (in other words everyone in your company must have access to the full picture on your customer)
5. Let customers help themselves
6. Help customers do their job
7. Deliver personalised service
8. Foster community

"Your customers are at stake. In this battle for electronic relationships, which has already begun, your customers are more important than your employees or 'bricks and mortar', because once lost they are so much more difficult to win back. Does anyone truly expect Barnes and Noble or Borders to catch Amazon?"

Chapter Four
Who's at war?

Who are the major protagonists?

If you visit www.mediametrix.com or netratings.com, you will see just how many of these electronic relationships the big 6 portals have already garnered. AOL, Yahoo, MSN, Excite, Lycos and Amazon have amassed between them close to 200 million electronic relationships with customers - that amounts to almost everyone on the internet as at the end of 1998. Wall Street is currently placing a value on a single electronic relationship at anything from $1000 to $7000 each.

Just compare two 1999 purchases: Ford's $8 billion purchase of Volvo with 400,000 new car sales per year with the $4.7 billion that Yahoo paid to purchase GeoCities with a database of 20 million electronic relationships. Over a 10-year period, Volvo's 400,000 sales or customers per year amounts to 4 million customers. If these customers change their cars every 2 years, Ford will have 2 million customers and if they change every 3 years, Ford will have 1.2 million customers. At a price of $8 billion, given the above, Ford paid between $4,000 and $6,500 for each relationship.

Yahoo paid a mere $235 for each relationship yet many observers say they paid too much for a loss making business …did they really? Consider also the $9.2bn that Comcast are paying AT&T for 2 million Mediaone customers' relationships, some $4,500 per relationship.

Now the portals are squaring off against each other. The battle is already underway on the Internet and the game plan is to capture at least 300 million of these two billion electronic relationships before 2002, when we anticipate a significant market correction, similar to 1929.

If Yahoo's market capitalisation stays on today's valuation this would give them a $300 billion capitalisation and the ability to buy just about any corporation in the world, with the exception of its four other rivals, Microsoft and General Electric. Yahoo we believe could capture 500 million electronic relationships (20% of the total available on the planet) taking them to $500bn market capitalisation as early as 2003.

If the Internet bubble bursts and the market drops by a factor of ten (historically unprecedented), Yahoo will still have $30 billion of market capitalisation to fall on. This is why Wall Street analysts are ignoring earnings to a large degree. This does not discount the fact that these Portals are in a battle for expansion and growth and in this battle, all growth is re-cycled for the war effort and big profits will not be seen until the battle ends. How long did it take the Romans to dominate Europe from their Portals in Rome?

As explained in the previous chapter, once these 6 Portals capture the 300 million electronic relationships each with individuals both at home and at work, they will provide a whole array of products and services. These are likely to include banking, telecommunications, financial services utilities and every conceivable retail item you care to name. If their customers require something they do not yet have, they will either buy it in at cost plus margins or acquire it using their market capitalisation.

The battle will filter across all sectors

Take the U.S. television and entertainment networks, CBS, NBC, News Corp's Fox, Disney, ABC, USA Networks and Time Warner. They have all been paired off already. CBS has teamed up with AOL and Netscape; NBC, which has been married to Microsoft Network (MSN) for some three years, recently spun off its own internet company to become a portal; News Corp's Fox has partnered with Yahoo; Disney in alliance with ABC and Infoseek launched Go.com; last but not least, Time Warner (parent of CNN, Time magazine and Warner Bros. and owner of 40% of cable TV systems in the U.S.) and AT&T linked via TCI with @Home who acquired Excite. [12]

Now let's move across to the Big 5 accountancy and consulting firms: PriceWaterhouseCoopers, Ernst & Young, KPMG, Deloitte & Touche and Andersens. These Portals are too big and complex and any change of firms is too complicated and hazardous to contemplate. So the Portals will soon enough decide with which firms they will want to align themselves. The same will apply to all sectors from airlines to zoos and all sectors in-between. Consider for a moment any industry you care to name, Automobiles, Music, Advertising, Retail, they all tend to end up with six dominating players. The six Portals are no different; the difference here is that by controlling the electronic relationship (in other words the Information) with the customer they marginalize all the other suppliers to that customer to the cost plus business. For this reason many brands will be forced to launch their own portals.

What do the experts say?

Chris G Charron, an analyst at Boston-based Forrester Research thinks Yahoo, Microsoft and AOL will come out on top. He likes AOL's strong revenue stream and its base of 17 million paying customers and its treasure trove of detailed demographic information. Yahoo's dominant position on the Web is allowing it to grab advertising revenue from its competitors. Microsoft is, of course, Microsoft, with theoretically unlimited resources, its Internet Explorer browser tie-in and a collection of strong commerce-oriented category sites, which will soon fall under the umbrella of its own portal wannabe, MSN.com. [Microsoft has another arrow in its MSN quiver, the CE windows operating system, to tie you via your palmtop or mobile phone or 'pocket portal', which we will cover later].

Boston technology consultant Patricia B. Seybold picked AOL and Disney as sure bets among the four or five "destinations" sites to survive to the year 2000. The other spots she says are up for grabs. Goldman Sachs analyst Michael Parekh suggests AOL/Netscape, Yahoo, Microsoft and Excite. Patrick Keane of Jupiter Communications, a Net market research company, says it's pretty simply: "Whoever spends the most and outbrands their competitors will win." [In 1998, we understand that Microsoft spent the most on advertising online]. Gartner Group Research Director, Patrick Meehan now counts Snap! (owned by NBC) on his list of portals most likely to succeed. James C Balderston, Jr., an industry analyst with Zona research declares that there is always a risk that in a bear market or an advertising recession, the portals newfound financial stability could disappear. Like the leaders in all emerging industries, Portals will have to manage both their expenses and their growth. Lastly, Bill Benedict, president of Greenwich, Connecticut-based Alpine Meridian Inc, an Internet strategy consultancy, contends that portals that don't stay in the top tier, will not go out of business. They will just have to adopt a more focused strategy to survive.[13]

Perhaps there is room for a second tier for the late arrivals at the party: Dell, Intel, IBM, HP, Cisco, Lucent, Nokia, Vodafone Airtouch, Oracle and Orange and countless others who haven't yet realised what the game plan is of the Portals. A recent wake up has come in Europe in the form of Deutsche Telecom (DT) and Italia Telecom. A yet unapproved merger between two state giants hasn't prevented DT from making a £10bn bid for the UK's mobile operator One-to-One (pocket portal) with 2.25m customers - yet again a market valuation at close to $5,000 each.

"Connect with your customers and suppliers electronically or get marginalized into the cost-plus business."

Chapter Five
No Portal, No Comment.

What about the brands?

Traditional brands and retailers will come under severe attack. Having a big brand won't be enough to save you unless you maintain direct electronic relationships with your customers and indeed your suppliers too.

By 2002, these Portals could be in a position so strong that they will be able to bulk buy any product or service from the lowest cost provider on the planet. We have already seen the arrival of zero-margin retailing from the likes of www.onsale.com and www.buy.com. Dixons have shown remarkable courage, cunning and fortitude by launching their "Freeserve" Portal and will likely follow it up with a free-PC.com equivalent to further strengthen their position. San Francisco-based Alexa Internet, which monitors traffic of visitors to Internet sites, places Freeserve in first position in the UK with 40,000 daily visitors from a member database of 1.5 million in just 6 months.

The critical ingredient for survival in the online world is the development and maintenance of direct electronic relationships with ALL your customers and ALL your suppliers. If you choose to advertise with the Portals to bring customers to your web site so be it, but make sure that you build your own direct and very personal electronic relationships of individuals, be they customers or suppliers, complete with their transactions history. In other words, make sure that in your organisation, ER stands for Electronic Relationships and not Emergency Room.

All industries go through a set pattern of growth, mergers and acquisitions and over a period of time the strongest and fittest survive. Take a look at the automobile industry: there are only the Big 6 left in the world. Look at the large accountancy/consultancy firms: there are only the Big 5 left in the world. Look at the airline industry: the world's major airlines belong to some five alliances, which for the sake of cost efficiency are rebranding themselves under one name. For instance "oneworldalliance.com" is the confederation of British Airways, American Airlines, Canadian Airlines, Cathay Pacific and Qantas. The Portals are here to do it again, with one exception . . . in half the time. [14]

The world perceives these Portals as the new kids on the block; they are upstarts and they appear ungovernable. They on the other hand want to project an image of integrity, trustworthiness, reliability and quality. They want you for all the values that you have over a long period of time painstakingly built in your brands. The predators have spotted their prey. [15]

There are essentially three ways to approach this problem: First, you can set up your own portal and have your own voice as it were (we calculate the cost of this at $1bn to $5bn). Second, you may decide no portal and therefore no comment and kow-tow to the Big 6 Portals. Third, you may decide you wish nothing to do with this new reality and just sit back and enjoy a slow death.

If you decide on the first route, it means you will set up your own portal and have direct relationships with your customers, suppliers and even shareholders. You will need to expand the range of your products and services. For example, Mercedes-Benz, which recently merged with Chrysler, have set up their own banking, credit cards, clothing line and mobile phones among others. In essence, you could be offering as much as your resources will allow you. This road offers large opportunities twinned with large dangers.

If you decide on the second route, it means you will end up being a cost-plus supplier to an existing Portal. Margins will be tight and it's a credit, inventory, warehouse and wholesale distribution business. Here the opportunities are limited, but the danger is always there; your Portal may go to someone else. Two very efficient organisations taking this route are Ingram and Tech Data both global computer products distributors, watch them widen their product and geographic portfolio over the next few years.

If you decide on the third option, we would like to leave you to meditate on a quote from Charles Darwin: "It is not the strongest of the species that survive, nor the most intelligent, but those most responsive to change."

Share and share alike

Writing on the subject of change, the news that California- based Free-PC.com hands over a free computer and free internet access seems to have taken the concept of attracting customers to a new high. In reality, the cost of giving away this product and service (freeware) pales in comparison to what Free-PC.com will gain. Free-Pc.com requires customers to complete their 10-minute questionnaire, to accept advertisements that surround their computer screen and to allow their searches and purchases to be monitored and analysed. Over a three-month period, Free-PC.com gained in excess of 1.2 million applications which translates into fresh, rich and immediate data on customer's current personal details, work, family, habits, interests, health and holidays and income and expenditure. Not only have Free-PC.com hit an oil well and amassed more information than they can deal with at present, they have also whetted he appetites of companies who want to advertise around those screens. Initially, the advertising dollars will help recoup their investment, but they will have a very rich database.

This is not the end. This is just the beginning. This move of Free-PC.com has made telecom and PC operators re-examine their strategy and they may well enter the market with a loss-lead to gain market position. For instance, IBM, Dell, Compaq (Altavista) and Gateway are Portals in waiting. Even the Internet service providers (ISPs), which rely heavily on their monthly subscriptions will have to move to the same model as Freeserve (not in the US though where local calls are free). There are dangers to this "Freeware" strategy. If all move to this strategy, the finite advertising, sponsorship and ecommerce dollars are likely to be squeezed. In the coming months, the battle for users will intensify against the telecom operators.

"In the future, telecom operators will have to play the new game of applications (portals), Internet Protocol and computers," says Kamel Maamria of A T Kearney, a management consultancy. He continues: "Traditional players will not be driven out of business as they have the customer base and the financial muscle [but their most profitable customers will likely be stolen first]. However, the new realities will lead to a new alignment of the right competencies, consolidations and fundamental alterations in the communications value chain that will lead to a new market structure that will bear little resemblance with the current market landscape."

These trends are already being seen in the ISP market. Most of the big European telecom operators have been actively buying independent ISPs.
"It is a way of getting closer to the customers of the future," says Robin Crowther, head of IP services at Cable and Wireless. [16]

"If you are not a Portal, you are a captive, cost-plus supplier to a Portal. Your margins will be tight and you are effectively in the credit, inventory, warehouse and wholesale distribution business. Here the opportunities are limited, but the dangers are ever present."

Chapter Six
Ecosystem: The 12 Principles
(*Originally* The E-Business Process)

By principle, we do not mean a scientific law or a religious doctrine. When we write or speak of principles, we mean a general rule, a guide, a component and a constituent part of a whole. As we explained in the introduction, the 12 Principles is not a process, it is an ecosystem. It is an ecosystem of organisations, each of which has four main communities. Each organisation will generally have a community of customers, a community of businesses, a community of stakeholders and a community of employees.

As the 12 Principles is a catalogue of the whole market, it is not just a guide and a constituent part of a whole. It has diverse uses in an organisation. It can be used to define clearly which board member is responsible for what areas. It can be used as a framework or language between the technical and the sales side of an organisation as well as between partnering organisations working on a project for the same client. We also use it primarily for training individuals. These are not the only benefits of the 12 Principles. The goal is to appreciate that the 12 Principles of E-Business are not a process, but an ecosystem. The real benefit for you is when you implement it and cross-fertilise it with, within and without your organisation. To do less would be missing the whole point of our offering. You will find an overview of the 12 Principles outlined below. For more information, please visit www.ecademy.com/.

Principle 1 is about learning. It is about learning all the 12 Principles of E-Business so that you can then cross-fertilise them with your business to derive maximum advantage from the new economy. It is not something you will add to your existing mental framework. It is to do with a complete change of perspective. It is a different environment. For many, it will mean unlearning old thinking habits in order to make room for new learning. You will learn about Information Providers, Research Companies, Investors and Venture Capitalist, Ecommerce Training Companies, Universities, Internet Lawyers, Taxation and Accountancy and Customer Behaviour.

Principle 2 is about planning. It is about whom you choose to work with in defining your E-Business Strategy. Choosing whom you partner with is a critical issue. Ideally, you need to select a company that owns a strategy and will motivate your department managers and provide guidance on each of the 12 Principles. The company you choose must not only understand the Internet and Ecommerce markets, but also your business, your customers and your suppliers. Ultimately, the maxim, 'failing to plan is planning to fail' is still valid in the new economy.

Principle 3 is about evaluating system software. This Principle is about evaluating your current software infrastructure system and then to decide what can be kept, consolidated and integrated and what needs to be abandoned. Software enables and controls the link between company information and its Internet site(s). This Principle is about understanding that link and why it is no longer necessary to regard the web site and company information as separate systems. Software will be the tool that constantly updates the prices on the main (legacy) database and simultaneously transports them to the site so customers and suppliers are immediately aware of the changes. This alone is an enormous task. For a company with old systems in place, it will involve the whole of their system and they will need to integrate many parts of the company, such as Sales, Personnel and Finance.

Principle 4 is about your company's communications infrastructure, which includes the hardware, the Intranet, the Extranet and the Internet service provider. All the computing power and data in the world is meaningless without a reliable and secure form of connection to the Internet and to the areas of the company that will be involved with it. Your company must also ask at the very start how much it is prepared to spend on hardware, what kind of web site it wants to offer and how many visitors it anticipates.

Domestic users know the frustration of waiting for data to download through the telephone line to their PCs. Online delays in Ecommerce are unacceptable because the customer will go elsewhere at a click of the mouse.

Principle 5 covers the area of security. This principle provides comfort to companies and their supply chains that their information is not open to abuse and comfort to their customers that their personal details are not open to abuse by the company or a third party. There are several types of security solutions such as, among others, the Public and Private Key Infrastructure (PKI) and Non-Repudiation Software. Passwords, verifications and digital certificates provide various layers of security that are increasingly difficult but not impossible to breach. What one has to bear in mind at all times is that there is no such thing as total security. Another aspect of security is that because it is based on fear and emotion, it can cloud clarity on this issue of security. Is it a real security issue or is it a perceived security issue?

Principle 6 focuses on payments. A Company needs to choose the type of process it would like to use in order to receive payments from its customers and to remit payments to its direct or indirect suppliers. Direct suppliers are those that supply core materials to the company and indirect suppliers supply ancillary materials such as office supplies. The process will vary depending on whether the company is in a business-to-business environment with monthly accounts or whether it is in a business-to-consumer market where payment is needed before delivery and also by the size of the transaction undertaken. Various payment mechanisms are covered such as Electronic Data Interchange (EDI) over the Web, Credit cards and Secure Electronic Transactions (SET), E-Wallets and Micropayments.

Principle 7 ensures that all the direct suppliers of the company are linked to the company's web site before customers begin to buy the company's products. The link is made in this order to avoid the risk of supplier shortage and inefficiency. In effect, the suppliers monitor their supplies with the company and replenish at set levels agreed with the company. On the Internet all companies look the same size. It is the way that they do business that makes the difference. The Internet user cannot see the flashy corporate building; it bypasses the facade. The link to suppliers can also include 'indirect' suppliers such as office and computer supplies. In this area, we also cover Enterprise Resource Planning (ERP) purchasing software for direct purchasing and Maintenance, Repair and Operation (MRO) purchasing software for indirect purchasing.

Principle 8 covers supplier portals. A supplier portal is nothing more than a single site from which a company can buy ancillaries that provide 'the materials' the employees need to make the operation work. A supplier portal will aggregate everything into one electronic catalogue, where goods can be ordered on one form, paid for and delivery expedited. The cost saving is fairly obvious: there is no need for multiple telephone calls, multiple forms or multiple payments. This will result in reduction in inventory costs and in cycle times. A supplier portal will also allow for near real time price comparisons and will support multi-currency transactions including the Euro. The supplier portal also makes the suppliers more efficient thus allowing them to offer better prices and better service to their customers.

Principle 9 covers inventory and logistics. In the recent past, if companies had a surplus of slow moving inventory, it might have organised a bricks and mortar sale or at worst sold it off for scrap. Today, it has the outlet of the Internet auction. There are numerous Web services that cater for business-to-business auction needs and often specialise in the type of goods sold, such as industrial and laboratory equipment, to computers and electronic parts and indeed across the whole business spectrum. The way a cyber auctions work is when bidders online tap in their bids on their keyboards. The bid is instantly recognised at the auction end, compared to other incoming bids and a response is generated. There are official closing times for online auctions, but in general terms an electronic gavel 'comes down' if there has been no bid for around two minutes. Some auctions last an hour, some up to a week or more.

Principle 10 comprises Selling Software. The Internet has no unions; it has no night and day and it has no statutory trading restrictions. It is a 24-hours-a-day, seven-days-a-week, 365-days-a-year, non-stop trading community. Past methods of selling have always had some form of restriction, either human, governmental, space or time, but the Internet never closes. In this salesman's dream, many things can go wrong. If goods are promised and not delivered, the Internet customer will not accept excuses; he or she will go elsewhere. Another common mistake is if the web site is difficult to understand or navigate. Research shows that difficult sites turn off typical end-users in the UK. Another one is where a site is overloaded with graphics and therefore slow to load onto the screen. We cover a wide array of software and tools.

Principle 11 embodies Customer Portals. A Customer portal is rather like a supermarket through which a company sells. It is in effect another distribution channel. One of the trappings of a portal is that it builds a 'community' and requires members to register. In this way, it builds up a demographic record collated in a database that develops into a valuable asset for business to tempt advertisers and e-Merchants. What makes portals attractive to retail consumers is their ease of use. Logging onto a portal on the Internet is rather like opening up a catalogue of products and services. The difference is the catalogue is huge with lists of category choices in groups of generic subjects such as business, travel, entertainment, money, news, people, health and education, shopping, politics, home and family and much more. Under each generic category you will find hundreds, if not thousands of sub-categories to investigate and explore. By following a hierarchical route, you can hyperlink to millions of web sites, which offer the product, service or information sought. Portals use search engine technology to help speed through the maze. They become route maps but in time once you have selected your preferred portal you will stick with them for pretty much everything. They will become a destination you hardly ever leave as their presence moves with you on all devices PC, TV, mobile phone, cable TV, bank ATM and so on.

Principle 12 is about personalisation, which means personalising goods, products, services and information to an individual's needs and wants. Although the Web is the technology of the future, yet paradoxically, it also enables a return to a very old-fashioned value: personalised contact with customers. An Internet site can be highly effective for monitoring and analysing the buying habits of customers, customising products and information to meet those habits and quickly responding to queries and requests. Internet sites can build and enhance relationships with customers through 'personalisation'. This is the Personalisation of the Electronic Relationships with your customers, suppliers and employees. An Ecommerce company can harness the power of personalisation through harvesting of customer profiles. Then, it can generate offers that it can send down the Email route - so called Push Technology - to software that helps manage Internet relationships. The power of personalisation lies in its ability to create loyalty. The customer that has spent time personalising the service at a particular site is less likely to switch to a competitor. Also, the ability of a company to provide a custom offering to its top accounts is central to the goal of cementing relationships and maximising the benefit of an Ecommerce business.

The 12 Principles are Open Source - They are free!
We welcome all individuals, partnerships and corporations to download Ecademy's 12 Principles and to build their learning on it. We also welcome all institutions, governments and enterprises. We, especially, welcome all educational and learning institutions too.

You are all welcome to work it by yourselves, amongst yourselves or in conjunction with us.

Chapter Seven
Winners and Losers

There is no magic formula. Conventional wisdom tells us that the strongest and the fastest will prevail, but that assumes there will be continuity. If there is discontinuity (say an interruption in technology such as we have now), 'the race is not to the swift nor the battle to the strong.' Ultimately, 'time and chance happens to them all.' If that were not the case, the rich and powerful dynasties and families, from the beginning of time, would still be the rich and powerful of today. Clearly they are not. Even institutions rise and fall: National Socialism in Germany, which was declared to last 1000 years - collapsed in ruins. Even Soviet communism imploded - without a battle. It appears that 'Time' and 'Chance' are what happens to all. That is not to say we should all give up and go home. If our ancestors did that we would still be in caves. We must balance our fears and our greed and temper our enthusiasm with caution. Let's look at some relevant history:

Deja vu?

The pattern from history seems clear if one looks at the similar growth trends in the Railroads in the 1850s, the Automobile in the 1920s and the Internet in the 1990s.

From 1850 to 1910 railroad growth in the US was phenomenal and its construction greatly stimulated the settlement and development of the West. In 1862, President Lincoln signed the Pacific Railroad Act, which authorised the building and operation of a railroad between California and Missouri. The Civil War (1862-65) in the US was prolonged because railroad gauges in the northern states (Union) differed from those in the southern states (Confederacy) and so transportation of troops was hampered. Compare that to how quickly Hitler was able to conquer Europe because he was able to transport his troops on European railroads, which had the same gauges.

In the 1920s, for example the single biggest force for growth was the tripling of auto production, along with a similar expansion of capacity in related industries such as steel, rubber and highway construction. The Standard & Poor's index for carmaker stocks more than quadrupled between 1925 and the spring of 1929. During the same period, the market as a whole rose 144%. But when auto sales hit their peak in April 1929 that signalled the end of the boom time for autos - and the rest of the economy. In the following four years, carmakers' stock prices dropped as far and as fast as they had risen. A few big players such as General Motors Corp. survived and even continued to be profitable, but many others, such as Auburn, Franklin and Pearce Arrow, disappeared in the following years, along with most of the money of the people who invested in them. [17]

That was not the end of history.

Railroads and Cars have changed our way of life irreversibly and for the great majority of us it would be difficult to imagine life without them. One could extrapolate easily how the next generation will view the phenomenal growth of the Internet and electronic commerce. We therefore consider it sensible to prepare everyone for a market correction in 2003.

Future

Just as in other industries, companies acquire or merge with suppliers or distributors or similar entities to secure sourcing of materials, to reduce costs or even for economies of scale, so it is with Internet companies that are scrambling to forge alliances to secure their future.

Electronic commerce (Ecommerce) is the end game for many Internet companies. They cannot do it alone. Take AOL, a portal, which acquired Netscape Communications, a Web browser, (the deal was announced in November 1998 and closed in March 1999) and soon after struck a far-ranging alliance between them and Sun Microsystems, a hardware company (it has been said that Scott McNealy at Sun architected the whole AOL-Netscape-Sun deal). The triumvirate of AOL, Netscape and Sun are tending to use EDS for their computer services and MCI Worldcom for their Internet (IP) network. This is an alliance prepared to go to battle to win the first prize and become an Ecommerce behemoth. AOL's initial objective is to lure retailers to its mall-like sites with a high volume of customer traffic and together with Netscape and Sun to offer them the software tools they need to build a new generation of cybershops. This is not the end of the alliances, but the beginning. Television networks are aligning themselves, NBC with Microsoft's MSN, CBS with AOL, ABC with Disney and Infoseek and CNN with Time Warner. Even big global consultancies and law firms will follow suit, as will many other global players in all sectors, who will recognise what they will gain from E-commerce.

Others are also forming alliances, but many are still "under construction"
and they are incomplete. Yahoo bought GeoCities and Broadcast.com and is working with Citibank First USA. Microsoft (and its MSN portal) has made alliances with AT&T, UK's BT, Japan's NTT and is looking to play a major role in the UK cable market through Telewest, NTL and probably Cable & Wireless. AT&T owns cable company TCI whose subsidiary @Home purchased Excite, the search engine. MSN will undoubtedly make a move to harness a US based computer services and hardware companies into its network, be it directly or indirectly. Disney bought Infoseek and emerged with "Go".

Now looking to the future, we believe that, even if there is discontinuity, Microsoft Network (MSN) and its cohorts of alliances will end up taking the Coca-Cola slot in the Portals sector and the Pepsi-Cola slot will be taken by America Online (AOL) and its cohorts. The rest will take their places in rote at the table of the Portals.

So who will be the losers? Picture this film scene:

" A mega-million dollar battle has been joined between the Internet big guns - the Portals. It is of such ferocity that when the winners survey the shattered debris on the battlefield, the strewn remains won't be those of dead customers or mortally wounded sales figures; the mutilated corpses will be those of the *brands*."

Not a pretty picture! The answer is the brands will be the losers. We have said this as a refrain throughout the book and we will say it again. Within three years, the Big 6 Portals will wield so much power that the question of the life or death of practically any brand on the planet will be in their hands.

So what can you do to save your brand?
The simple answer is don't delay; change fast. For a more elaborate answer, we would like to highlight a selection of the crucial rules and instructions that authors Carl Shapiro and Hal Varian offer us in their book *"Information Rules"*.

"Technology changes. Economic laws do not." and "Focus not just on competition but also on your collaborators;"

Information technology is rushing forward, seemingly chaotically and it is difficult to discern patterns to guide business decisions. But there is order in the chaos.

Let's look back at the telephone companies of the mid-1890s. Bell's key patents had just expired; the U.S had just emerged from a depression, causing independent (non-Bell) companies to proliferate. By 1903, Bell companies controlled less than half the telephones in America. What led to the emergence of a dominant national company, the Bell System? Oddly enough, the key was long-distance telephone service; oddly because long-distance service was only 3% of all calls. But the writing was on the wall.

Local phone companies were finding it very profitable to combine adjacent town and extend their reach. In urban areas, businesses were willing to pay a great deal for long-distance service. The Bell system faced a fundamental strategic issue: would it be better to restrict long-distance access to its affiliates or open the network to independents? At first Bell allowed only its affiliates. By 1900, Bell hit upon the winning strategy: open up to non-affiliated companies that met Bell's technical and operating standards and that were not direct local competitors. Soon this reversed the tide of competition and in time the Bell system grew to dominant position under the corporate name of AT&T, until its break-up in 1984.

Many of today's companies face interconnection issues not unlike those facing AT&T a hundred years ago. Under CEO Michael Armstrong's leadership, a re-energised AT&T appears to be emulating that old Bell strategy that made Bell so powerful in the past.

"A wealth of information creates a poverty of attention." and " Information is like an oyster: it has its greatest value when fresh."
"Information is costly to produce but cheap to reproduce" but also "Price information according to its value - not its cost."

Now that information is available so quickly, so ubiquitously and so inexpensively, it is not surprising that everyone is complaining of information overload. Nobel prize-winning economist Herbert Simon said, " A wealth of information creates a poverty of attention." The real value of information comes in locating it. It is no accident that the most popular sites belong to search engines, those devices we use to find the information we are seeking. In real estate, it is said that there are three critical factors: location, location and location. Any idiot can establish a Web presence; the problem is letting people know about it.

Timeliness is highly valued by some customers and of little importance to others. Offer different versions of your products and service and price it accordingly. "Information is like an oyster: it has its greatest value when fresh;" and "Price information according to its value - not its cost."

This is especially true of 'strategic' information, such as information about stock market or interest-rate movements, where individuals possessing the information have a strategic advantage over those lacking it. Nevertheless cost and value are two completely different issues. Let's look at the story of The Encyclopaedia Britannica (EB).

EB has been regarded as a classic reference work for more than 200 years. As a classic it has commanded a premium price: a few years ago, a hardback set of thirty-two volumes cost $1,600. In 1992, Microsoft decided to get into the encyclopaedia business and bought rights to Funk & Wagnall's (F&W), a second-tier encyclopaedia that was selling to supermarkets. Microsoft used the F&W content to create a CD, called Encarta, with some multimedia bells and whistles a user-friendly front end and sold it to users for $49.95. EB also went into the electronic age offered to libraries at a subscription rate of $2,000 per year. EB continued to lose market share. In 1995, EB offered the home market an online subscription of $120 per year, but to no avail. In 1996, EB offered a CD version for $200, but still nothing really moved. That same year a Swiss financier, Jacob Safra, bought EB, disbanded its sales network of 110 agents and 300 independent contractors and started aggressive price-cutting. EB now sells its CD for $89.99 matching Microsoft Encarta.

"Information is costly to produce, but cheap to reproduce." The dominant component of fixed costs of producing information is sunk costs, costs that are not recoverable. Personalise your product and personalise your prices.

"Keep control of information and databases by using standard formats," and "Loyalty programs will proliferate."

Users with massive information encoded in a specialised format are vulnerable if and when they require new hardware or improved software to work with data. In these situations, a key question is whether the information can easily be ported over to another system. You must ask yourself what are the costs of transferring the information and what aspects of the information would be lost in transfer. A good example is a consumer who has built up a library of CDs and then a new audio technology appears on the scene. The consumer is locked in CD format. In this case the information cannot be transferred, making it important for anyone selling equipment that reads new formats, such as DVD, to make equipment backward compatible - that is capable of reading CDs as well.
One way for users to limit these switching costs is to insist on employing standardised formats and interfaces.

More and more businesses will use loyalty programs, as customer information becomes more detailed and more widely available. Complementary suppliers will co-ordinate their programs, much as hotels and airlines now cooperate in their repeat-buyer programs. With online trading, these possibilities will explode. With loyalty-induced programs, customers can easily calculate the costs they bear when switching vendors. Some vendors will buy credits from their competitors to induce them. The online bookstore Amazon has a nice twist to its loyalty program. In the 'Associates Program', anyone who recommends a book on his or her web site can add a link to Amazon that can be used by those who wish to purchase the book. In exchange, Amazon offers a referral fee of between 5% and 15% of the purchase price. In March 1998, there were more than 35,000 Amazon associates and by the following year there were in excess of 100,000 associates. This gives Amazon a potent weapon in its battle with Barnes & Noble, who retaliated and so the battle ensues.

"Positive feedback makes larger networks get larger." and "Build alliances to ignite positive feedback in the network economy"

The next historical example is more recent: the adoption of colour television in the United States. The colour television technology in the U.S. is known as the National Television Systems Committee (NTSC). Critics insist that NTSC really meant "Never Twice the Same Colour". This system was formally adopted in 1953 but the story has many lessons.

The story begins with the inauguration of black-and-white television transmission in the U.S. on 1st July 1941. At the time RCA, the owner of NBC Television, was also a leading manufacturer of black-and-white sets and a powerful voice in radio and television. But the future of television was to be colour, which had first been demonstrated by Bell Labs in 1929. Throughout the 1940s CBS Television was pushing for the adoption of the mechanical colour system it was developing. RCA urged the FCC to wait for an electronic system. A major obstacle with the CBS one was that their colour sets could not receive existing black-and-white broadcasts.

Despite the drawback, the FCC adopted the CBS system in October 1950. The RCA system was not ready. As David Sarnoff, head of RCA, said, "The monkeys were green, the bananas were blue and everyone had a good laugh." This was a political triumph for CBS, but they were poorly placed to take advantage of this victory, as they did not even have manufacturing capability. Luck entered the picture. With the onset of the Korean War, the U.S. Government ordered a suspension on the manufacture. Both CBS and RCA were pleased as it gave them time. By the time the ban was lifted in June 1952, the RCA system was ready and consensus in support for it had formed at the NTSC. In March 1953, CBS raised the white flag, noting that with 23 million television sets in American homes, compatibility was important. NBC and CBS invested in colour transmission quite quickly; by 1957, 106 out of 158 stations in the top 40 cities had the ability to transmit colour programs. But things moved slowly. RCA had spent $130 million to develop colour TV with no profit to show for it. The missing ingredient was content. Then, as now, a killer app was needed. The killer application of 1960 was *Walt Disney's Wonderful World of Color.* On the Internet seemingly little has changed because Information is still the killer application.

The lessons we can learn from this story are as follows. First, adoption of new technology can be painfully slow. Second, the collapse of CBS shows that first mover advantages need not be decisive. Third, the colour television experience highlights the importance of building alliances. Fourth, this example shows the dangers of sitting back and assuming that you can maintain market dominance just because you control the current generation of technology or have a large installed base. [18]

"The race is not to the swift or the battle to the strong, Nor does food come to the wise or wealth to the brilliant
Or favour to the learned; but time and chance happens to them all."
Ecclesiastes 9:11

Chapter Eight
What's next?

A Flashback

Just as the printing press was the cause that broke the Roman Catholic Church's hegemony over Europe, the computer and internet will break the Welfare State, so say authors James Dale Davidson and William Rees-Mogg in their book, *The Sovereign Individual*.

Current Affairs

It is no secret that democracy has been relatively rare and fleeting in the history of governments. They quote William Pfaff: "Democratic political systems are a recent affair, in historical terms. They had a brief existence in Greece and Rome, afterward re-emerging in the 18th century, fewer than 200 years ago . . . A cycle of repudiation may now have begun again."

Dale Davidson and Rees-Mogg suggest that when the Berlin Wall fell, it was not just Communism that collapsed; its fraternal twin, Democracy, also fell. Compared to Communism, the democratic welfare state was in fact a more efficient system. But compared to a genuine laissez-faire enclave like Hong-Kong, the welfare state was inefficient. They suggest that an obvious alternative would be to privatise governments, so they would run efficiently and have electronic plebiscites, where a representative fraction would cast ballots.

Tomorrow's World

"When the age of the Information War finally arrives, it is unlikely that the antagonists will only be governments. A company like Microsoft certainly has a greater ability to conduct Information War than 90% of the world's nation-states." The end of an era is usually a period of intense corruption, and they give examples of the Clinton' scandals and the frauds in the European Commission. This is a time when the forces of progress battle with the forces of reaction and violence inevitably ensues. They advance the notion of "The Age of the Sovereign Individual" is now upon us and with it a return to the medieval concept of a city; today's gated communities mushrooming everywhere. In the next century, they envision the creation of a world superclass, perhaps of 500 million very rich people, with 100 million being rich enough to emerge as Sovereign Individuals.

A selection of the implications and strategies they proffer are listed below:

1. Citizenship is obsolete: Customers are in.
2. U.S. citizenship will convey the greatest liability to becoming a Sovereign Individual.

3. Reside in a country other than that from which you hold your first passport.
4. Violence will become more random and localised
5. Areas of opportunity and security will shift.
6. The fastest growing and most important new economy of the next century will not be China, but the cybereconomy.
7 Where possible, all businesses should be domiciled offshore in a tax-haven jurisdiction. This is particularly important for Web sites and Internet addresses.
8 The death of politics will mean the death of central bank regulation. Cybermoney will become the new money of the Information Age. This means the death of inflation and real interest rates will rise.
9. Cognitive skills will be rewarded as never before. It will be more important to think clearly, as ideas will become a form of wealth.
10. The growing danger of crime, embezzlement and theft will make morality and honour among associates more highly valued than during the Industrial Age. [19]

Another perspective is presented by influential futurologists, Ira Matathia of Omnicom and Marian Salzman, Director of Brand Futures at Young & Rubicam, the world' third largest advertising agency. We highlight excerpts from their book: _NEXT? A Vision of Our Lives in the Future._

Living in the Digital Age

By 2010, all barriers to adopting the Internet will fall. Why? The most compelling reason is that computers are no longer about technology. They're about something far more important: community and communicating. Do we know how a car works, but we still drive it. Do we know how a telephone works, but we still use it. We are told that the killer app for most Latin Americans won't be online research or shopping; instead it will be online chat - a natural outlet for cultures that stress social interaction.

Loving and Lusting

Even our loving and lusting is in for some change; we will have a new intimacy, an electronic intimacy [reference the film "You have Mail" with Tom Hanks and Meg Ryan]. That's not all. There's even silicon sex. It appears that Philips Electronics in the Netherlands plan to introduce a 'singles chip' that's designed to unite compatible lovers. The chip, which is small enough to be concealed in an earring or tie pin, can be programmed with such information as likes, dislikes and personality traits. When in a singles bar, nightclub or other social arena, the chip is designed to scan the room for other singles chips and beep if it locates a compatible profile.

Family styles and @Home.

New approaches to home design and community development will take place. By the year 2000, the mother-father-two kids' family will represent fewer than

25% of the total American households. As a result, there will be flexible housing, where people will choose to buy only the space they need and can afford. The home will become totally wired. Honeywell's TotalHome Control System integrates security, temperature, lighting and appliance controls into one wall-mounted keypad for both new and existing homes.

Personal Lives

Everybody wants our patronage and our money and so they will entertain us to get it. One-stop family entertainment centres, gambling and holidays. There will even be virtual travel, which is effectively a ten-minute mind-cleansing virtual holiday.

How We Work: the Future of Offices.

Virtual offices are in because they are more cost efficient. Space cost money. Staff will be asked to give up their private space in exchange for the freedom to work where they like. Change of this magnitude, we are warned, evokes a broad variety of personal reactions and consequences. Their connection to each other will come via Intranets or internal company networks are based on the same technology as the global Internet. Cordoned off from the public via software known as firewalls, Intranets allow employee access, while blocking unauthorised users. Some analysts anticipate this will lead to the next big leap, which will be the creation of the virtual corporation. Already, for instance, Pharmaceutical giant

Eli Lilly has created an Intranet that links approximately 16,000 workers.

How Commerce and Media Work Us: Next Persuasion

Barriers to Ecommerce will continue to fall. As obstacles such as fear of credit card fraud, the need to return goods and fear of big brother are addressed, Ecommerce will blaze away. It has an entrepreneurial edge, but it doesn't mean stratospheric increases in sales. Eshopping requires a different way of thinking and one that may not come naturally to larger companies. Traditional retail is already finding that competition from online retail is making life tougher and online commerce has a 4% higher profit margin than traditional sales avenues, according to Forrester Research. Ernst & Young's recent 'Internet Shopping' study found that 69% of online shoppers surveyed base their buying decisions, in large part, on their familiarity with the company. That's why the Portals are so focused on establishing themselves as the new brands.

You are What Influences You

78% of respondents to a U.S. study by Forrester Research said they make time for PC use by spending less time in front of the TV. Viewers are not giving up their favourite programmes, but they are cutting down on aimless TV channel surfing. They are starting to realise that the Internet and the Information it contains is more stimulating then TV.

Digital printing, which weds computer-generated content with high-speed copiers, eliminates the economies of scale associated with offset printing. Using Xerox DocuTech printers, publishers Simon & Schuster produces more than 125,000 customised books a month. Implications are that this will bring to an end to 'out of print' books. The book you are reading now has been produced this way taking a mere two hours to be produced once you ordered it from the web site. This process historically has taken anything from four to twelve weeks. Thus there is no need to hold a stock of books and furthermore the content of these books can be updated monthly on the fly.

360 Degree Branding

Marketing strategies today must be holistic. The basis of the theory is simple. Everything communicates. Every business today must compete in two worlds: the physical marketplace and the online marketspace. Authors Matathia and Salzman offer us their 10 realities of the next millennium:

1. If you know the marketplace, you can own the marketspace
2. Any company with a site automatically becomes a global company.
3. New product announcements on the net will generate immediate demand.
4. Geekspeak is the newest international language - forget Esperanto!

5. The distinction between news and gossip is becoming blurred
6. Everyone has the potential to be influential in cyberspace.
7. Privacy will become a very rare commodity
8. New technologies are giving small and midsize companies far greater access to consumers than ever before.
9. The homogeneity of traditional media images and messages are breaking down as ethnic and minority groups gain a voice on the net
10. The Internet is turning the population into creators of content as opposed to mere consumers of it.
[20]

In another story, Marks and Spencer is already working on a version of technology whereby shoppers could save the time and trouble of trying new clothes for size. This technology works as follows: customers enter a scanning booth where beams of intense white light play over their bodies. The scanner uses the reflections to build up a detailed dectronic image of the customer's body. Then the customer slots a smart card containing their body scan results into a device capable of communicating with clothing tags by radio waves or infra-red light. As a customer walks around the shop, the device is pointed at racks of clothes and singles out garments with measurements matching those on the smart card. [21]

We would like to add our own particular predictions for the next century:

1. The electronic dollar (Edollar or Eurodollar) is inevitable and will become the global currency in cyberspace.
2. Europe will have a single currency, a single parliament and a single president.
3. The period 2000-2030 will not only be the Electronic Commerce generation but also the European Community generation
4. The pocket portal, an electronic device combining the sum of the PC, mobile, Internet and portal, will carry your personal data shadow, which will effectively act as your "electronic butler". We discuss this in more detail in the following chapter.
5. Electronic Commerce will ultimately result in one global currency, one language, one government, one set of laws and one President. Don't ask us when - but never say never!

"Imagination is more important than knowledge"

Albert Einstein 1879-1955

Chapter Nine
Where's my Pocket Portal?

In the previous chapter we touched on the subject of a "personal data shadow" and an "electronic butler". In this chapter, we define what they are and how they will be used.

Let's suppose that as part of your work you were assigned a human butler. This butler would need to know as much about you as you feel comfortable in releasing to him. The more he knows about you the better he can serve you and over time his service may or may not improve. With your electronic butler, memory size, human error and personality failings are not an issue and therefore the service will be superior.

What is a Personal Data Shadow?

It is exactly what it says. It is personal; it is your complete data and it shadows you wherever you go. The personal data shadow is your personal database and it holds all your information most importantly <u>all</u> your transactions. The information held encompasses personal, professional, financial, medical, dental, social, travel, purchases, sales and everything else. The personal data shadow will be available on your PC desktop, your mobile phone, your cable TV or whatever other instrument is created to house it. Yes it could be the refrigerator. The critical thing is that all your personal data is with you at all times, wherever you go and whatever you do.

What is a Pocket Portal?

The pocket portal is the physical device that holds your personal data shadow and acts as your connection to the Portal. When you request say theatre tickets on your pocket portal, it is the Portal that will execute your request. It will also act in conjunction with your personal data information (which would include, for instance, your seating preference in theatres and your vodka and tonic at half time) and arrange for the tickets to be delivered to you.

These are words we have given to concepts. The technology is already available such as personal digital assistants, mobile phones, automobile PCs, kiosks and automatic teller machines. What has not been developed is the planning and marketing of the concept of a personal data shadow. It will come and sooner than even we can predict.

Smart cards?

Earlier on we gave two examples, which we can now re-introduce to explain more clearly what we are advocating. The first was that of Philips Electronics' 'singles chip' or smart cards that's designed to unite compatible lovers. The small chip, concealed in an earring or tiepin, is programmed with your likes, dislikes and personality traits. When you are out in a singles bar, nightclub or other social arena, the chip will scan the room for other singles chips and beep if it locates a compatible profile.

The second example was about a smart card that Marks and Spencer are working on which holds complete information of your body dimensions so that when you go shopping you place the smart card in a scanner they provide and just point it at the selection of clothes you like. Your scanner will single out garments with measurements matching those on your smart card. Your smart card will be located inside your Pocket Portal.

There are as many uses as your imagination will allow. Think where else in your life that you could use this facility? Let's consider your holiday travel? You beam the selected information that you wish to reveal to your Portal (who is also your travel agent) through your pocket portal device. That information is passed to the airline and hotel so they know exactly what to have ready for your arrival. Just suppose you have an infant, would it not be nice to have all the little things that could upset you on holiday dealt with instantaneously? For example, a supply of nappies, a hot water thermos flask, a cot, your various favourite drinks. Perhaps for the other members of your family, tickets to a particular show or sight in that destination or even a renowned restaurant that's been recommended to you. We'll let you make your selection.

It's not the device; it's the information

A central point to keep in mind is that the personal data, and what it does, is the most important. The technology or pocket portal is subservient to it. Technology will constantly evolve: on introduction to the market place, some will fail outright, some will have relative success and a few will excel. Of those that excel, each will have its ascendancy - just look at the telephone, radio and television - and then they will make room for the next technological advance. But that does not mean the death of these excellent devices: they will be resurrected in a different format. Now it's the PC's ascendancy that's challenged.

"The era of the personal computer is over, " declared IBM on 25th March 1999. Lou Gerstner, the chief executive of IBM, made the claim in a letter to shareholders. The reasons he gave are that firstly, "the Internet" and other electronic networks are taking over the work done by personal computers and secondly, sales of PC would be badly hit by the proliferation of "Non-PC Internet devices." [22] The personal computer that Gerstner refers to is the desktop. All computer devices are personal computers in our view, whether they are desktop, notebook, laptop, personal digital assistants, mobile phones, kiosks or automatic teller machines. All these devices are also personal pocket portal computers. The era of these personal computers is not over: it is just beginning!

"Computing will come in a vast array of devices aimed at practically every aspect of our daily lives. Unlike PCs, these devices will be simple and convenient. Think divergence instead of convergence. Nokia, Ericsson, Motorola and at least five other phonemakers are developing Web phones. HP, IBM, Sun Microsystems and Sony amongst others are preparing a host of new gadgets from palm-size scanners to the underlying chips and software that will power these devices. What's feeding this explosion of innovation? You guessed it. The Internet." [23]

We highlight BusinessWeek's list of the new post-PC products, which in fact will all be in your pocket portal:

- Qubit wireless web tablet - to read online news over morning coffee
- Alcatel webtouch phone - to check movie times
- HP Capshare handheld - to save magazine articles
- IGS's Neopoint or QualComm's PDQ - to send Email by mobile phone
- NTT's wristwatch-size mobile phone - for Granny
- 3Coms Palm organiser - to call up favourite snapshots
- Diamond Multimedia's Rio - lets you play music downloaded from the Internet
- Tivo's set top box - will automatically store your favourite shows

Killer Information Application

All the above are nothing short of gimmicks: the real scramble is for the Killer Information Appliance (killer app), which brings us back to the Personal Data Shadow. This killer app is a device, which acts as the "bell" to call Jeeves, your electronic butler. If you happen to have your account with say AOL, you will call up AOL and tell it what you want and AOL will find it and return the information or request.

Over time, all your personal details and transactions are recorded: your groceries and toiletries list, your travel, hotel, airline preferences, your likes and dislikes, your personality type, your allergies and ailments and even your psychoses and neuroses. Remember this information is private and confidential and it can reside in different locations and in different devices. The database that records this information becomes intelligent. It starts to learn and then to breathe as it were and even starts to make suggestions and recommendations to you. It becomes your personal data shadow or your electronic butler. Do we really need a personal data shadow? The answer is yes for a very simple reason; we are becoming so busy both at home and at work, with so much communication that any service that can make the business of transacting our daily lives easier will be adopted. For instance, questions on an individual's medical history, which is already resident on a Portal database, will only need to be answered once and will be automatically updated as and when events occur.

Infomediary and Portal

This "pocket portal" or "AOL" or "Personal Data Shadow" is only one part of the equation. The Portal that you belong to that provides ALL your services is in fact nothing less than the Infomediary that we touched on in Chapter 1. It is this infomediary that is bringing you what you want and need.

In an environment of unlimited selection and access to information, the scarce resource becomes customer attention. Customers still face one unyielding constraint: they still only have 24 hours a day. Where and how they choose to use this time will have enormous economic consequences. With limited time and unlimited choice, customers will likely focus their attention on providers that best understand their needs and can, as a result, maximise their return on attention by delivering, highly tailored bundles of products and services.

Today brands are largely product-centric, which means they are statements about the vendor's. Brands say in effect: "Buy this product, it is high quality". In an environment where return on attention becomes a key measure of performance, a new kind of brand will emerge: a customer-centric brand, which is an information, brand (a Portal). Customer centric brands have two components. First, they assure that vendor understands the individual customer better than anyone else and secondly they promise the customer that the vendor can tailor products and services to the individual customer's needs better than anyone else. [24]

Vast corporations, used to imposing their own corporate brands on the world through advertising and PR will find themselves having to listen to what these infomediaries or portals have to say on behalf of customers.

It is this infomediary that is bringing you what you want and need. This infomediary or portal will represent you, the customer, and it comes between you and the vendors. The Portals are the new Information Brands and as we have said many times will become the new global public utilities. If you find this difficult to believe, you are not alone.

"Heavier-than-air flying machines are not possible."
Lord Kelvin, 1895

"I think there is a world market for maybe five computers."
IBM Chairman Thomas Watson, 1943

"640,000 bytes of memory ought to be enough for anybody."[25]
Bill Gates, 1981

Chapter Ten
Can it still go further?

Tools change human perception and thinking

Before we can project to the future, we need to review the past and understand how human perception and thinking has evolved with each emerging technology.

In the Agricultural age, a farmer did not understand abstract concepts; it was all about survival. Abstract concepts developed when man started to read and write. As we move into the Information age, the very materials of technology, through video and film, will also change how we perceive our world, as is explained in the following story.

In the early 1930s, a young psychologist, Alexander Luria, was sent to Uzbekistan by the Soviets to record how people thought, before they introduced collectivisation and formal education. Luria found that when the pre-literate Soviet peasants were shown a round geometric figure and asked to describe it, they said they saw a plate, a bucket or the moon, but not a circle. Instead of a square, they saw a door, a house or a board for drying apricots. After being drawn four objects:

hammer, saw, log and hatchet they were asked to group them. Their response was that they are all alike; the saw will saw and the hatchet will chop. The emergence of an abstract category like "tool" owes much to literacy. [26]

The medium is the message

The point we are making here is that just as writing changed the way we see and interpret the world about us, the same will undoubtedly happen as we travel deeper into the Information age. "The medium - not the content - is the message," wrote Marshall McLuhan in 1964. "It is the medium that shapes and controls the scale and form of human association and action." He proclaimed the end of the linear age (transmission of thought by the lines on a page or one-to-one communication of speech) and the arrival of a New World, which offered total experience through the electronic media. The computer, said McLuhan, "promises by technology a Pentecostal condition of universal understanding and unity." [27]

Special Superfast Chips

Industry experts predict that by 2005, the convergence of computers, telecommunications and consumer electronics will push demand for digital-signal processing (DSP) to ten times what it is today. There is a battle in this sector between the four leading U.S. chipmakers: Texas Instruments, Lucent Technologies, Motorola and Analog Devices. DSP chips that can understand speech will replace touch pads and push buttons on all kinds of products - including VCRs that you can program by telling them what to record.

DSP may just as well stand for "digital sensory perception". They are the nerve cells that connect electronic devices to the real world. They are honed to deal with sounds, images, pressure, temperature, electrical currents and radio waves - all this at blinding speed. The new chips will turn cars into concert halls. These superfast chips are paving the way for many new applications; copy machines, microwave ovens and TVs could lose their push buttons and sprout microphones. [28]

How does this link in to the Battle of the Portals and your personal data shadow? The answer is it will convert communication between the customer and portal from the tedious mode of writing to requests by speech, touch and vision.

"Nerve cells" and "digital sensory perception" lead us straight to Bill Gates' book entitled *Business @ the Speed of Thought: Using a Digital Nervous System*. "Business is going to change more in the next 10 years than it has in the past 50 years," writes Gates. In a recent interview, he said that most companies don't realise that the tools to accomplish these changes are now available to everyone; the heart of the most business problems are information problems because almost no one is using information well. Here on the edge of the 21st century, the tools and connectivity of the digital age give us a way to easily obtain, share and act on information in new and remarkable ways. A digital nervous system is the corporate equivalent of the human nervous system, providing a well-integrated flow of information to the right part of the organisation at the right time.

Information on numbers cannot remain the preserve of the senior managers only, says Gates. Companies should spend less time protecting financial data from employees and more time teaching them to analyse and act on it. The system should notify them of unusual developments, according to criteria set, such as, if an expense item is out of line. To begin creating a digital nervous system, you must develop an ideal picture of the information you need to run your business and understand your markets and your competitors. Then develop a list of questions to which your answers would change your actions. You will know you have built an excellent digital nervous system when information flows through your organisation quickly and naturally as thought in a human brain. It's business at the speed of thought. [29]

Business at the speed of thought invariably leads us to "computers that can think and learn faster than humans". This is also known as 'organic' computers. If this sounds frightening or ludicrous, imagine what medieval man must have thought of the ideas of tanks and helicopters that Leonardo da Vinci drew in detail, even before the technology was created? He understood the power of image: "If the poet can kindle love in man, more so the painter, as he can place the true image of the beloved before the lover."

MIT's Ray Kurzweil is the world's leading authority on artificial intelligence. He states, "The continued exponential growth of technology in the first two decades of the twentieth century matched that of the entire nineteenth century. It is in the nature of exponential growth that events develop extremely slowly for extremely long periods of time, but as one glides through the knee of the curve, events erupt at an increasingly furious pace. And that is what we will experience as we enter the twenty-first century."

Kurzweil states that the brain, which is an organ, is not only neurological, but it is also perfectly mathematical. It can process naughts and ones faster than any other machine in the world. In 1996 a computer called "Deep Blue", a chess-playing computer, beat Gary Kasparov, the worlds master chess player and champion. Kurzweil studied what Deep Blue was doing and has calculated that by 2030, an equivalent Intel microprocessor at that point will outperform the human brain.

Kurzweil makes his own predictions for the future as follows:

1999

He believes there will be some disruption and a lot of litigation, but the Y2K (Year 2000) is unlikely to cause the massive economic problems that are feared. Computers are dependable, dumb and docile. We suspect there will be pockets of disruption particularly in less advanced economies.

2009

- People have at least a dozen computers on and around their bodies (*pocket portals*) allowing them to conduct financial transactions and entry into secure areas.
- Cables are disappearing and short-distance wireless technology emerges.
- Interaction with animated personality to conduct a purchase or make a reservation is like talking to a person using a videoconferencing, except that the person is simulated (*pocket portal*).
- Learning at a distance, for example lectures and seminars in which participants are geographically scattered, is commonplace (*The Ecademy*).
- Telephone communication is primarily wire-less. Users can instantly download books, magazines, newspapers, television, radio and movies *(onto their pocket portals)*.
- Despite occasional corrections, the years leading to 2009 have seen continuous economic expansion and prosperity due to the dominance of the knowledge content of products and services. The greatest gains continue to be in stock market values. Price deflation concerned economists in the early years, but they quickly realised it was a good thing. It seems that only Alan Greenspan at the Federal Reserve truly understands this.
- At least half of all the transactions are conducted online. Intelligent assistants, routinely assist with finding information, answering questions and conducting transactions (*pocket portals*).

- Lifetime medical patient records are maintained in computer databases *(and on your pocket portal)*.

2019

- Computers are now largely invisible. They are embedded everywhere: in walls, tables, chairs, desks, clothing, jewellery and bodies.
- Significant attention is paid to the personality of computer-based personal assistants *(pocket portal)*, with many clones available.
- Most twentieth century paper documents of interest have been scanned and are available through wireless technology.
- Most adult human workers spend the majority of their time acquiring new skills and knowledge (*The Ecademy*)
- The vast majority of transactions include a simulated person; often there is no human involved.
- People are beginning to have relationships with automated personalities and use them as companions, teachers, caretakers and lovers *(pocket portal)*.
- The existence of the human underclass continues as an issue. Old controversies persist regarding issues of responsibility and opportunity.
- Most flying weapons are tiny and some as small as insects; under research are microscopic flying weapons.
- The expected lifespan has now substantially increased to over 100.

- Machine intelligence has been programmed to maintain a subservient relationship to the species that created it.

2029

- A $1,000 (in 1999 dollars) unit of computation has the computing capacity of about 1,000 human brains.
- Automated agents are now learning on their own
- The vast majority of communication does not involve a human
- Basic life needs are available for the vast majority of the human race

2049

- The common use of nanoproduced food, which has the correct nutritional composition and the same taste and texture of organically produced food, means that the availability of food is no longer affected by limited resources.

2099

- There is no longer a clear distinction between humans and computers.
- Most conscious entities do not have a permanent physical presence
- The goal of education and of intelligent beings, is discovering new knowledge to learn

Kurzweil concedes that these steps are not inevitable. The human species together with its technology may destroy itself before achieving this step. Destruction of the entire evolutionary process is the only way to stop the exponential march of the Law of Accelerating Returns. [30]

"Capital isn't scarce, vision is."
Michael Milken

U.S. Financier and philanthropist

The Nation, 1991

Conclusion

Customer acquisition for the New World of Ecommerce is what's at stake in The Battle of the Portals. From the immediate perspective, it is no longer about economies of scale, but economies of scope. The relationship with the customer must go deep. Deep in the sense that the Portal that understands the customer very well can provide the customer whatever products or services they want or need, instantly, constantly, and even be pro-active in this service. The depth of the relationship that Portal and customer develop will be continuous and will be enhanced by the unrelenting technological advance of the "pocket portal" communications device. The customer relationship will become an Electronic Relationship with an Information Brand.

From the distant perspective, just as the development of the cities in Europe was a feature of the break-up of feudalism, the development of Internet will be a feature of the break-up of the way we transact business tomorrow. Marshall McLuhan emphasised that the medium shapes and controls the scale and form of human association and action. Just as the pre-literate 1930s Soviet peasants in Uzbekistan would have had to learn to read and write to understand abstract thought, we also must learn the new language of the Internet if we are to understand how to grow and prosper in this new community.

It is not just the business world that will be impacted but also our whole way of life. "The world, led by the United States, is in the third great crisis in Western education," says Neil Postman, then New York University professor of communications studies. The first took place in Athens in 5 BC, when an oral culture was replaced by an alphabet-writing culture, giving rise to the writings of Plato. The second came with the invention of the printing press, giving rise to the writings and influence of John Locke. The third, he holds, "is happening now, in America, as a result of the electronic revolution." [31]

While technology changes, economics laws and marketing laws do not change. Management guru Peter Drucker once said, "Because its purpose is to create a customer, the business enterprise has two – and only two – basic functions: marketing and innovation. Marketing and innovation produce results; all the rest are costs." [32] The essence of the Internet business is "marketing" and "innovation" and as such it will produce results. There may be delays, there may be interruptions and there may be market corrections, but the pincer movement of 'marketing for customers' and 'pocket portal innovation' will advance relentlessly.

From the spiritual perspective, all technology has its good and bad uses. Take the ubiquitous table knife. It can be used to cut one's food and it can also be used to kill a human being. It is not the technology that is evil, but what is in a man's heart. Life is about constant change;

nature changes through the seasons and humans start dying from the moment they are born. Man is a creature of habit and when he is comfortable, he does not want to change. Man also wants time to stop and not go forward because he is afraid of change. Therein lies the evil, not in the technology. Some argue that many will lose their jobs, families will break up and people will starve. Did not the Luddites use that flawed argument? They were uncomfortable and fearful of change, like many of us. They had nothing to fear then, just as we have nothing to fear now.

The Internet may be compared to the "New World" and The Ecademy likened to the "Mayflower" ship that's carrying information pilgrims to the New World. In December 1620, when some 41 of the adult passengers gathered in a cabin and formulated and signed the Mayflower Compact, all the adult males were required to sign it. It was the first constitution written in America and it protected and provided for this new settlement. Similarly, the 12 Principles are formulated to protect you, to assist you and guide you in this New World of E-Business.

"The dogmas of the quiet past are inadequate to the stormy present. The occasion is piled high with difficulty and we must rise with the occasion. As our case is new, so we must think anew and act anew . . . Fellow citizens, we cannot escape history." [33]

U.S. President Abraham Lincoln, December 1862
Annual message to Congress

Table 1

Market Capitalisation of Internet Companies

	Feb-99	Jun-99	Sep-00	Apr-01
	$bn	$bn	$bn	$bn
Microsoft	n/a	408	n/a	302
AT&T Corp	159	169	116	78
eBay	n/a	23	n/a	9
Cisco	n/a	177	n/a	99
MCI WorldCom Inc	146	167	90	53
AOL Inc	80	115	129	173
Vodafone	59	65	235	190
Airtouch(Vodafone)	55	65	0	0
Yahoo Inc	35	33	62	8
Amazon.com Inc	19	19	16	3
Excite Inc	6	sold	sold	sold
Lycos Inc	6	4	8	sold

Courtesy: Flemings Asset Management and Thestreet.com

Table 2

Media Metrix
Top 50 Digital Media/Web Properties.

Unique Visitors (000)

Name	Feb-99	Jul-00	Apr-01
AOL Network	38,414	62,545	85,186
Microsoft Sites	30,866	50,298	90,597
Lycos	29,187	32,119	50,144
Yahoo Sites	31,075	49,045	87,504
Go Network	21,897	21,848	24,170
GeoCities (Yahoo)	19,926	n/a	n/a
Excite (AT&T)	18,081	27,115	38,141
Time Warner/CNN	12,715	16,365	15,016
Amazon	10,516	15,383	19,760
Altavista	9,709	17,391	19,756
NBC	8,551	n/a	17,548
Xoom Sites (NBC)	9,730	n/a	n/a
Broadcast (Yahoo)	8,870	n/a	n/a
Netscape (AOL)	18,666	n/a	n/a

Reference Notes

Chapter One

1. Martin Butler & Thomas Power, *The E-Business Advantage*, pg. 63
2. Patricia Seybold, *Customers.com*, pg. 123
3. Richard Tomkins, "Old father time becomes a terror", FT Weekend March 20/21, 1999 (4)
4. John Hagel III and Marc Singer, *Net Worth: Shaping Markets When Customers Make the Rules.*

Chapter Two

5. Geoffrey Colvin, "How to be a Great eCEO", Fortune Magazine, May 24, 1999
6. *Microsoft Encarta '95*, Interactive Multimedia Encyclopedia
7. *The Sovereign Individual*, by James Dale Davidson and William Rees-Mogg, Chapter 4, page 82
8. *The Internet and World Wide Web: The Rough Guide 1998* by Angus Kennedy
9. *Information Rules: A Strategic Guide to the Network Economy* by Carl Shapiro and Hal Varian, Chapter 7, page 184

Chapter Three

10   Larry Black, Sunday Business, London: article entitled, "Battle-lines drawn in web power struggle", 28 February 1999.

11   Patricia Seybold, *Customers.com: How to create a profitable business strategy on the Internet.*

Chapter Four

12   Larry Black, Sunday Business, London: article entitled, "Battle-lines drawn in web power struggle", 28 February 1999.

13   Amy Stone, Patrick Lambert and Linda Himelstein, Businessweek, New York: article entitled, "The Battle of the Portals: Who will be left standing in the fiercest contest in cyberspace?", 28 August 1998

Chapter Five

14   The Ecademy Newsletter, "The Battle of the Portals", Surrey,
15 February 1999

15   Thomas Power, "Ignoring the Portals could change your Brand's life ... or end it." *Marketing Week* magazine, March 1999

16   Christopher Price, *Financial Times*, FT Telecoms, "Give away PCs may herald fresh initiatives", London, 18 March 1999, page VII.

Chapter Six

www.theecademy.com

Chapter Seven

17. Michael J. Mandel, *Businessweek* magazine, "The Internet Economy: As the Web turbocharges growth, it's bringing fresh risks.", New York, 22 February, 1999
18. Carl Shapiro and Hal R. Varian, *Information Rules: A Strategic Guide to the Network Economy*, Harvard Business School Press, 1999

Chapter Eight

19. *The Sovereign Individual*, by James Dale Davidson and William Rees-Mogg, Chapter 10
20. Ira Matathia & Marian Salzman, *NEXT?: A Vision of our Lives in the Future*
21. Paul Nuki, "Talking clothes get our measure," *The Sunday Times*, 21 March 1999

Chapter Nine

22. Andrew Butcher and Chris Ayres, "IBM says era of personal computer is over," *The Times*, London: 26 March 1999
23. Peter Burrows, Andy Reinhardt and Heather Green, "Beyond the PC" - Special Report: *BusinessWeek,* 8 March 1999

24	John Hagel III and Marc Singer, *Net Worth: Shaping Markets When Customers Make the Rules.* page 235
25	*"The Age of Spiritual Machines"*, Orion Business Books, London, 1999, page 169

Chapter Ten

26	Mitchell Stephens, The Rise of the Image and the Fall of the Word, Oxford University Press, New York: 1998, page 19
27	J Herbert Altschull, *"From Milton to McLuhan: The Ideas behind American Journalism"*, Longman, New York, 1990, Chapter 55
28	Otis Port and Paul C Judge, "Chips that mimic human senses,"*BusinessWeek*, European edition, 7 December 1998
29	"Speed gives life to digital nervous system," *Financial Times*, London, 18 March 1999.
30	*"The Age of Spiritual Machines"*, Orion Business Books, London, 1999
31	J Herbert Altschull, *"From Milton to McLuhan: The Ideas behind American Journalism"*, Longman, New York, 1990, Chapter 55

Conclusion

32	*The Hutchinson Dictionary of Business Quotations*, Helicon Publishing, London, 1996, page 34 ("costs")

33 Lord Charnwood, *Abraham Lincoln,* (1917) Dover Publications, Inc., New York, Chapter 10, page 327